KFK KINGFISHER KNOWLEDGE

LIFE IN ANCIENT
ROME

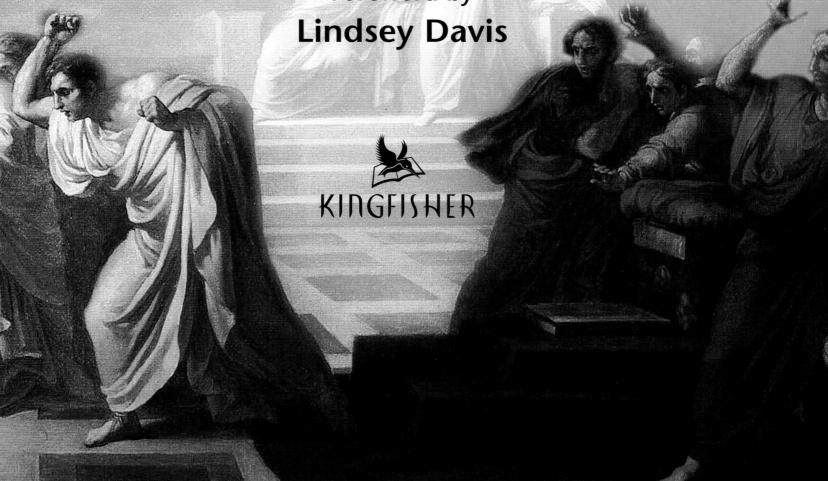

KFK KINGFISHER KNOWLEDGE

LIFE IN ANCIENT ROME

Simon Adams

Foreword by
Lindsey Davis

KINGFISHER

Publishing manager: Melissa Fairley
Senior designer: Peter Clayman
Consultant: Dr Thorsten Opper, The British Museum
Picture research manager: Cee Weston-Baker
Senior production controller: Lindsey Scott
DTP co-ordinator: Carsten Lorenz
Artwork archivist: Wendy Allison
Proofreader: Sheila Clewley
Indexer: Diana LeCore

KINGFISHER

Kingfisher Publications Plc, New Penderel House,
283–288 High Holborn, London WC1V 7HZ
www.kingfisherpub.com

First published by Kingfisher Publications Plc 2005
10 9 8 7 6 5 4 3 2 1
1TS/0706/PROSP/MA(MA)/128MA/C

ISBN: 978 0 7534 1199 5

GO FURTHER...

INFORMATION PANEL KEY:

 websites and further reading

 career paths

 places to visit

NOTE TO READERS

The website addresses listed in this book are correct at the time of going to print. However,
due to the ever-changing nature of the internet, website addresses and content can change.
Websites can contain links that are unsuitable for children. The publisher cannot be held
responsible for changes in website addresses or content, or for information obtained through
third-party websites. We strongly advise that internet searches should be supervised by an adult.

Contents

Foreword

I wonder what comes to your mind when somebody mentions ancient Rome? For most of us, our first thought is likely to be an image of a legionary soldier, stern-faced in his red tunic, segmented breastplate and helmet. Then we may think of straight roads, carefully laid-out towns, central heating, baths, the excitement of chariot races and gladiators. And what powerful event could be more frightening and destructive than the famous eruption of Mount Vesuvius at Pompeii, which gave us vivid archaeological remains – and which may be due to erupt again at any time.

I write novels about the ancient Romans, so I have had to learn about all of these things. It has been fascinating and surprising. Although the Romans were often very different from us, in many ways they were strikingly similar. We find it upsetting that they owned slaves, and that animals and men were killed in the arena as a public sport; in fact, there were a few Romans who also disapproved – just as they might have found things we do peculiar. They believed in privacy at home, so perhaps they would think the internet was intrusive, and I'm pretty sure they would say they handled relations with foreign countries better than we do. Otherwise, so much about them is familiar. They were keen fans of home-makeovers. They had celebrity chefs. I like the fact that, unlike in some ancient societies, women and children were valued and loved in the Roman world. Life in Roman cities seems particularly modern; for instance, on every street corner, they had snackbars – the direct ancestors of our sandwich bars.

The Romans lived a long time ago, but their legacy is strong, especially in the countries which formed part of the Roman empire, which stretched from Scotland (though not all of it!) to Libya, and from Spain to Syria. In all those countries the Romans had a great hand in establishing how people live today, how they organize themselves politically, how they think and speak. There are visible monuments to remind us of their presence all that time ago. Knowing the layout of Roman roads has helped me find my way around modern Britain in my car. I once went down a sewer under the Roman Forum, which was still being used as a stormwater drain (yes, it was rather worrying to be there). How many things we build today will still be working in 2,000 years' time, I wonder? That's even though the Romans gave us what we think of as a very modern building material – did you know that concrete was a Roman invention? They even invented a kind that would set under water, for use in harbours and aqueducts.

People are intrigued by the Romans, because they are such an important part of our own history. We want to learn more about them. I hope you will enjoy finding out about their city and their achievements – so now read on!

Lindsey Davis

Lindsey Davis – award-winning author of the Falco Roman detective novels

CHAPTER 1

From city to empire

According to legend, twin brothers were set adrift on the River Tiber in Italy and were rescued by a she-wolf, which looked after them until a shepherd found them. When they grew up, the twins began to build a city upon a hill. But they quarrelled, one killed the other, and the survivor became king of the new city, which he named after himself. He was Romulus,

the city was Rome, and these events took place in c.750BCE. It is a wonderful tale, but it is just a story, with little basis in fact. The exact truth about the founding of Rome is lost in ancient history, but we do know that from this hill grew a kingdom, and then a republic, and then an empire, that stretched across the whole of western Europe, North Africa and the Middle East.

The founding of Rome

There are two stories about the founding of Rome, one a legend, the other fact, yet both have merged to form a single story. The legend tells of Aeneas, son of the Greek goddess Aphrodite, who escaped from the burning city of Troy in c.1250BCE after its capture by the Greeks. Aeneas fled to Italy, where he married a princess and began a line of kings. Two of his descendants – Romulus and Remus – were twin brothers.

The legend

The twins' great-uncle Amulius wanted to be king, so he ordered his soldiers to throw Romulus and Remus in the River Tiber. But they were found by a she-wolf that cared for them until a shepherd took them in. When the twins grew up, they killed Amulius and around 750BCE built a new city on the Capitoline Hill. But the twins quarrelled and Romulus killed Remus. He then became king of the city, which he named Rome.

The facts

In reality, archaeologists believe that Rome began around 800 as a collection of huts built by the Latin peoples on the Palatine and other hilltops next to the Tiber. These villages grew to form a single city that spread over all seven hills around 750. The Latins were one of many tribes in the area, alongside Sabines, Etruscans, Samnites and Greeks.

▼ The twin boys Romulus and Remus were suckled by a she-wolf, whose carved and sculptured figure appears throughout Rome and is a symbol of the city's foundation.

▲ The kindly shepherd Faustulus and his wife took charge of Romulus and Remus from the she-wolf. Faustulus and his family were favourite subjects of later painters and sculptors.

Stealing Sabines

According to legend, Romulus soon realized that his tribe did not have enough women, so he asked the neighbouring Sabines to a festival and stole their women. The fact that Sabine influence was strong in early Rome gives this story some element of truth, especially as the two tribes agreed that Latins and Sabines would alternate as kings of Rome.

The kings

The three kings after Romulus are shadowy figures ruling over a city of wooden buildings, but the fourth, Tarquinius Priscus (ruled until 597), was an Etruscan who seized power around 616. New buildings were built of stone, and the marshy Forum area was drained and laid out as a public square.

▼ Romulus offered Rome as a sanctuary for refugees, but this attracted more men than women. He got around this problem by holding a new festival, the Consualia, and inviting the Sabines. The Romans seized and married the Sabine women while the Sabine men were distracted playing games.

▼ The seven hills of Rome were an ideal site on which to build a city, as they were close enough to the sea to reach it by boat down the Tiber, but far enough away to be safe from pirates.

The Roman republic

The seventh king of Rome was the tyrannical Etruscan Tarquinius Superbus (535–510BCE), or 'Tarquin the Proud'. The Roman historian Livy (59BCE–CE17) tells us that in 510, after the Roman noblewoman Lucretia was attacked by Tarquin's son Sextus, a group of Romans rebelled against the king and expelled him and his family from Rome. In his place, the Romans set up a republic.

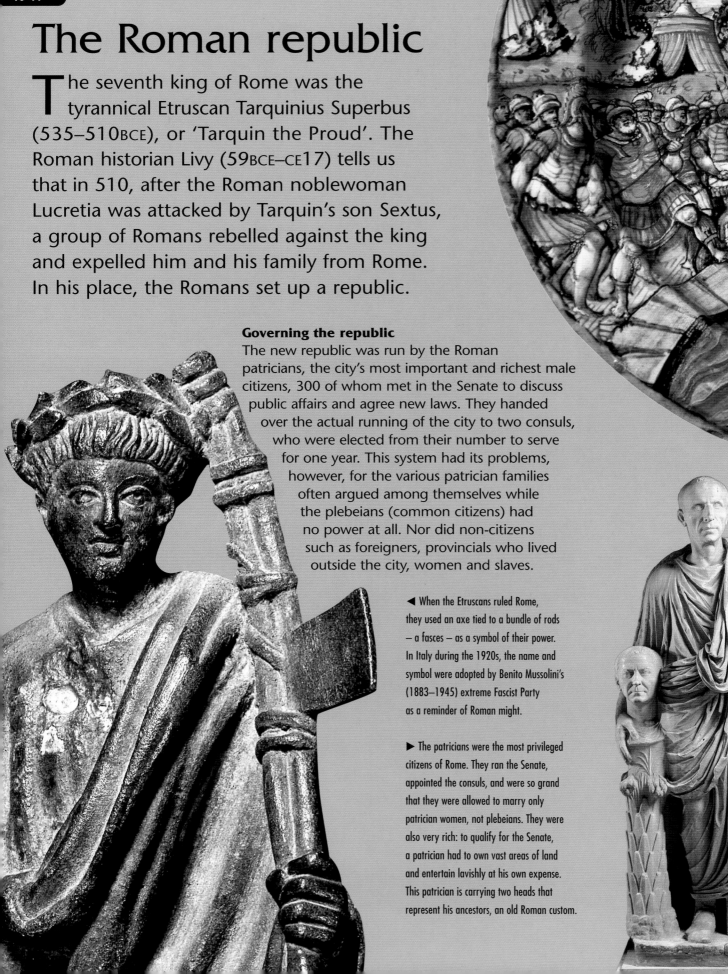

Governing the republic

The new republic was run by the Roman patricians, the city's most important and richest male citizens, 300 of whom met in the Senate to discuss public affairs and agree new laws. They handed over the actual running of the city to two consuls, who were elected from their number to serve for one year. This system had its problems, however, for the various patrician families often argued among themselves while the plebeians (common citizens) had no power at all. Nor did non-citizens such as foreigners, provincials who lived outside the city, women and slaves.

◄ When the Etruscans ruled Rome, they used an axe tied to a bundle of rods – a fasces – as a symbol of their power. In Italy during the 1920s, the name and symbol were adopted by Benito Mussolini's (1883–1945) extreme Fascist Party as a reminder of Roman might.

► The patricians were the most privileged citizens of Rome. They ran the Senate, appointed the consuls, and were so grand that they were allowed to marry only patrician women, not plebeians. They were also very rich: to qualify for the Senate, a patrician had to own vast areas of land and entertain lavishly at his own expense. This patrician is carrying two heads that represent his ancestors, an old Roman custom.

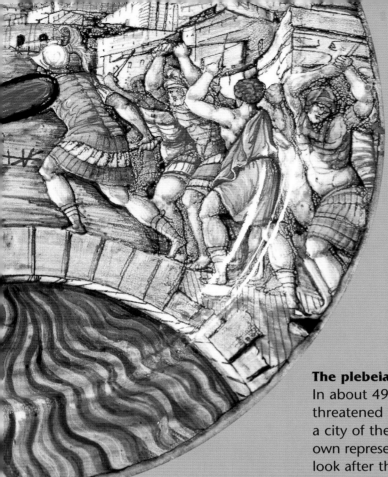

▲ After Tarquinius was expelled from Rome, he received help from the nearby Etruscan city of Clusium. Its army tried to cross the wooden bridge over the Tiber into Rome, but were stopped by a soldier, Horatius, who held them off while the Romans destroyed the bridge behind him. Once the city was safe, Horatius jumped into the river and swam to safety.

▶ Roman women, whether they were patricians or plebeians, had no power in the republic. They could not vote or take part in public affairs, nor could they hold any office. They could, however, influence their husbands and sons, giving some of the women power behind the scenes.

The plebeians revolt

In about 494, the plebeians threatened to leave Rome to set up a city of their own. They elected their own representatives, the tribunes, to look after their interests. The tribunes defended the plebeians and their property, and could summon public meetings to agree plebiscita (new policies). The Senate reluctantly agreed to these radical changes.

Power to the plebeians

In 450, after further plebeian riots, the ten tribunes collected all their previous decisions together in the Twelve Tables, which set out the plebeians' rights. After renewed conflict, the law was changed in 367 to allow plebeians to become consuls. In 287, plebiscita became binding on the whole population, even if the Senate disagreed.

▶ Although they formed the vast majority of the population, the plebeians of Rome had few rights. They formed the main workforce in the city, constructing the buildings, running the shops and public baths, and defending the city against attack.

◄ From 343–341BCE, and then again from 327–304 and 298–290, the Romans fought the warlike Samnite hill tribe of southern Italy. Eventual victory over the Samnite warriors (left) saw Rome expand its territory over the Apennine mountains to the Adriatic Sea.

▼ Pyrrhus's army consisted of 25,000 soldiers, 3,000 horses and 20 elephants – the first time the Romans had ever come across these creatures. Despite Pyrrhus's two victories, the Roman army was finally able to overcome him at Malventum, south of Rome, in 275BCE.

The conquest of Italy

In the 5th century BCE, Rome had become an important city in central Italy, but it was surrounded by enemies and had to fight for its survival. Within 200 years, Rome controlled the whole of the Italian peninsula and was ready to dominate the entire Mediterranean Sea.

Under siege

Rome's closest neighbours were the fierce Aequi and Volsci tribes who lived on the hills to its east and south. Once these were defeated by 400BCE, Rome was able to expand further, capturing the Etruscan city of Veii to the north after a ten-year siege in 396. Rome was immediately threatened, however, by the Gauls, a Celtic tribe from central Europe who had settled in northern Italy. In 390, they attacked the city and burned most of it to the ground before retreating north with their booty.

► As the Gauls attacked and burned Rome in 390BCE, the Romans retreated to the temple on top of Capitoline Hill. According to legend, the Gauls tried to storm the hill one night, but disturbed the geese that were kept there. Their cackling woke the Roman soldiers up just in time for them to fight off the Gauls and save the city from complete devastation.

Protect and expand

Once the Gauls had left, the Romans rebuilt their city, protecting it with the 10km-long Servian Wall. In three lengthy wars, they defeated the Samnites of southern Italy but then came into contact with the various Greek cities around the coast. The Greeks of Tarentum appealed for help from King Pyrrhus (318–272) of Epirus – a kingdom in northwest Greece – who arrived in southern Italy with a large, well-trained army in 280.

A pyrrhic victory

Pyrrhus defeated the Romans twice in 279, at Heraclea and Ausculum, but his losses were so great that he observed that 'another victory like that, and I'll be ruined'. We still talk today of a pyrrhic victory, one that is gained at too great a cost. Eventually the Romans defeated Pyrrhus in 275, capturing Tarentum three years later and the whole of southern Italy by 264.

The Roman army

The key to the success of the Roman republic, and the reason it grew into a great and powerful empire, was the mighty Roman army. This army was a formidable fighting force, well-equipped, highly trained and disciplined, and more than a match for any other army of its day. Indeed, many people consider the Roman army to be the most successful fighting force in history.

A legion

The main part of the army consisted of infantry units known as legions. Each legion was made up of eight-man conturberniums grouped together in tens to form a century, each commanded by a centurion. Confusingly, therefore, a century did not contain the 100 men one would expect – the number had been reduced to 80 to make it easier to control and command a century in battle. Six centuries combined to form a cohort of 480 men, and ten cohorts – nine with 480 men each, the tenth and leading cohort with 800 men – combined to form a single legion.

▲ Around CE250, the infantry was joined in battle by a heavily armoured cavalry force. Emperor Constantine (ruled 307–337) divided the army into limitanei (frontier troops) and comitatenses (the field army) 50 years later. Both armies contained cavalry and infantry (see 2nd-century CE relief, above).

▶ An imperial Roman soldier wore body armour made of thin metal strips tied together with leather straps and worn over a coarse woollen tunic. Around his waist he wrapped his badge of office – a cingulum (belt) with metal pendants – and wore hobnailed caligae (military sandals) on his feet. In his hand he carried a sharp thrusting spear, later replaced by a heavy pilium (javelin). Each legion had its own distinguishing banner.

Into battle

Each legion included more than
100 horseback messengers, a doctor,
cooks, builders, engineers and
a catapult maker, for the legion had
to build its own bridges to cross
a river, as well as construct forts, roads
and siege engines. A fully staffed
legion contained about 6,000 men.

► Traditionally, the army
recruited its legionaries from
among Rome's land-owning
citizens. In 107BCE, the consul
Gaius Marius (157–86)
changed the army by accepting
volunteers who were paid by
the state. This change led to the
development of a professional
army able to fight lengthy
wars in distant places.

The auxiliaries

Only Roman citizens could become legionaries.
Alongside them were the non-Roman auxiliaries,
recruited from subject peoples within the empire.
Some of them, such as the Syrian archers, formed
specialist units that fought with their own weapons.
Although they served for longer periods than
legionaries and were less well paid, they did
have the incentive of becoming Roman
citizens when they left the army.

Fighting the Carthaginians

While Rome controlled the Italian peninsula, the real power in the region was Carthage, a North African city in what is now Tunisia. Carthage was a huge maritime empire in the western Mediterranean and Spain, and had grown rich on trade and commerce. Over the course of three lengthy and often bitter wars, Rome and Carthage fought for domination of the Mediterranean.

▼ Carthage was almost completely destroyed by the Romans in 146BCE. The remains we see today are of a later Roman city founded by Julius Caesar (see pages 20–21) 100 years later, although some of the original city has recently been excavated.

The First Punic War

In 264BCE, the first of three wars broke out over control of Sicily, the large island off southern Italy. Carthage had a powerful navy, but the Romans had few ships and were inexperienced sailors. Luckily, they obtained an old Carthaginian warship and copied it to build their own fleet.

▲ The three wars between Rome and Carthage were called the Punic Wars, as the Carthaginians originally came from Phoenicia in Lebanon: Punic is Latin for Phoenician. The Carthaginians were skilled craftworkers, making terracotta heads of local people, often sporting fashionable nose rings, as well as jewellery and other items.

▲ Carthaginian warships were built for speed and stability. Sailors drove them through the water using one or often two tiers of oars, while soldiers and quantities of arms were carried on deck. The Romans copied this design to build their own fleet. This relief is c.1st century BCE. The tower would have housed a 'drawbridge' used to board enemy ships.

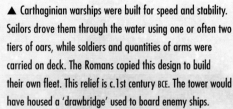

The Roman fleet

Twice the new Roman navy defeated the experienced Carthaginians, but twice the Roman fleet was destroyed in storms. Eventually, in 241, the Romans delivered the knockout blow off the Aegates islands, west of Sicily. This success brought Rome the island of Sicily – its first overseas territory.

The Second Punic War

Carthage remained a threat, and when it began to rebuild its empire in Spain, a second war broke out in 218. This second war was dominated by the Carthaginian general Hannibal (see pages 18–19). When the war ended in a Roman victory in 201, Rome acquired the entire Carthaginian empire in Spain.

The Third Punic War

By now, Carthage had lost its empire and posed no threat to Rome. But Rome was still concerned about its former enemy: one Roman senator threatened that 'Carthage must be destroyed' at the end of every speech. The third and final war broke out in 149. A huge army attacked and defeated Carthage in 146, burning the city to the ground. Its people were sold as slaves, and the ground was sown with salt so that nothing would ever grow.

Hannibal

The quickest way to get from Carthage to Rome is by boat, a short hop across the Mediterranean from North Africa to Sicily and southern Italy. But when war broke out between the two cities in 218BCE, the Carthaginian general Hannibal (247–183) had other ideas. He took the long land route through Spain and France across the Alps into northern Italy. And just to be different, he went by elephant – the ancient world's tank!

▲ The goddess Cybele, from Phrygia in Asia Minor (Turkey), was introduced to Rome and adopted in 204BCE – just before Scipio's successful invasion of Carthage – because an oracle prophesied that she would bring victory to Rome against Hannibal.

▼ Hannibal's army consisted of 40,000 men, several thousand horses and about 40 elephants. These creatures were the now extinct North African breed, smaller than the usual African or Indian elephants and measuring only 2.5m from ground to shoulder. We do not know the exact Alpine route Hannibal took, but when he emerged in the Po valley, Italy was at his feet.

Crossing the Alps

Hannibal set out from Spain. He travelled along the Mediterranean coast and, once in Gaul (France), headed north up the Rhone river valley and then east into the Alps. The Romans had a large army guarding the coastal route, so he decided to catch them by surprise by entering Italy through their Alpine 'back door'.

◄ Publius Scipio (236–184BCE) was a brilliant military commander from a great military family: his father and his uncle had defeated the Carthaginians in Spain in 215. Scipio's daring strategy of attacking Carthage itself in 204 ended Hannibal's campaigns in Italy by forcing him to return home, while his victory at Zama brought victory to Rome in 202.

The end of the war

As the war dragged on, it looked as if it would end in stalemate. The Romans, however, wanted victory. In 209, the Roman general Scipio attacked Hannibal's brother Hasdrubal (d.207) in Spain and drove the Carthaginians out. Scipio then took the initiative and in 204 he invaded Carthage itself. The still undefeated Hannibal was forced to return home to defend the city. The end came in the North African desert where, in 202, Scipio defeated Hannibal at Zama. Carthage lost its entire fleet and all but a small piece of land surrounding the city because of the peace settlement. Rome now controlled the Mediterranean.

Crushing victories

For the next 15 years, Hannibal won victory after victory against the Romans, decimating two large armies at Lake Trasimene in 217 and Cannae in 216, where at least 30,000 Romans lost their lives. Large parts of Italy defected to Hannibal but he was unable to capture Rome itself. The Roman general Quintus Fabius Maximus (c.275–203) avoided large battles and gradually wore Hannibal down, cutting him off from his home base and depriving him of supplies.

Julius Caesar

On 10 January 49BCE, the Roman general Julius Caesar (100–44) stood on the banks of the Rubicon river, the boundary between Gaul (France) and Italy. He had just completed the conquest of Gaul and had crossed the English Channel twice to subdue the Britons. Caesar was at the height of his powers, and had a huge army at his side. But he knew that to cross the Rubicon was to declare war against the Roman republic he so faithfully served.

The mighty generals

Ever since the defeat of Carthage (see pages 16–17), Roman armies had expanded the empire eastwards into Greece, Asia Minor (Turkey) and Syria. But these victories had come at a cost, for the conquering generals now wanted political power as well. In 88BCE, two of them, Cornelius Sulla (c.138–78) and Gaius Marius (see page 15), fought for control of Rome; after Marius's death, Sulla killed his supporters and ruled Rome as dictator from 82–80.

The fateful decision

In 70, another strongman, Pompey the Great (106–48), became consul and allied himself with Julius Caesar. But the two men eventually fell out and the Senate ordered Caesar to return home from Gaul without his army. On the banks of the Rubicon river, Caesar made the fateful decision to ignore the order and seize power for himself.

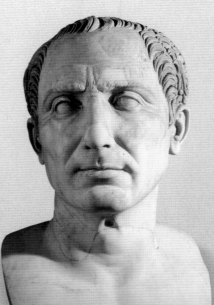

► Julius Caesar (modern bust, right) was a brilliant military commander who was immensely popular with his troops. He was also a fine orator and author, writing a celebrated seven-volume history of his wars in Gaul. After his death (see painting on pages 2–3), Caesar became the official title of all Roman emperors, a name that lived on as 'Tsar' in Russia and 'Kaiser' in Germany.

Dictator for life

Once in Rome, Caesar crushed all dissent, defeating Pompey in 48 and putting down rebellions in Spain and North Africa. Caesar was an inspired leader – he reorganized the government and taxation systems, and introduced the 365 and one-quarter day Julian calendar we still use today. He tackled poverty by freezing rents and cutting debts, and gave grants of land to poor people and ex-soldiers. In February 44, he made himself dictator for life, but his enemies resented his huge power and popularity and plotted to kill him. A month later, two of his former friends, Cassius (d.42) and Brutus (c.85–42), led a group of senators to assassinate him on the Ides (15) of March.

▼ We still do not know exactly where the Rubicon river was, but it is usually identified with the River Uso, which rises in the eastern Apennine Mountains and flows into the Adriatic Sea north of Rimini. The river formed the boundary between Gaul and Italy; by leaving his own province of Gaul, Caesar lost his right to command his army and was thus acting illegally.

Antony and Cleopatra

The death of Julius Caesar in 44BCE (see pages 20–21) launched a period of civil war in the Roman republic that lasted until 30. Three years later, the republic became an empire when Caesar's adopted son Octavian (62BCE–CE14) became the first emperor. But those troubled years also saw one of the greatest love affairs of all time, between Mark Antony (83–30), Caesar's right-hand man, and Cleopatra, the last ruler of Egypt (69–30).

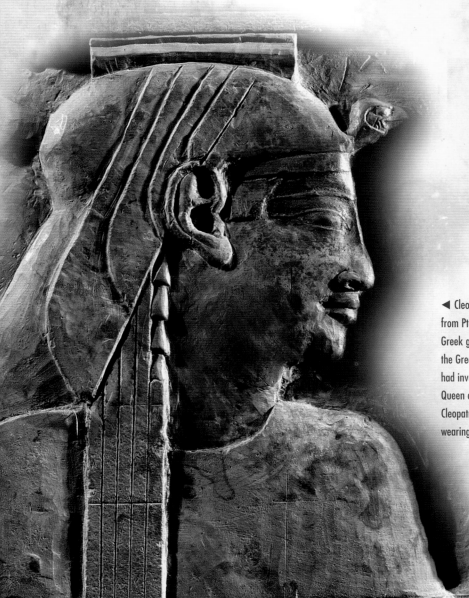

◄ Cleopatra was descended from Ptolemy, one of the Greek generals of Alexander the Great (356–323BCE), who had invaded Egypt in 332. Queen of Egypt from 51–30, Cleopatra is shown here wearing the royal headdress.

Divide and rule

After Caesar's death, control of Rome was disputed between Octavian, who wanted peace with Caesar's enemies, and Mark Antony, who wanted revenge. The two agreed to work together to defeat Brutus and Cassius, Caesar's assassins, which they did at Philippi in Macedonia in 42. They then agreed to share power, Octavian taking the western half of the empire, Antony the eastern. Octavian spent the next ten years securing his power before finally confronting Mark Antony.

▲ Mark Antony (above) was consul with Julius Caesar and had the support of the army and people of Rome after Caesar's death. But he was outwitted and defeated by the more able leader Octavian.

Cleopatra

After Julius Caesar had invaded Egypt in 48, Cleopatra became his lover and bore him a son, Caesarion. She went with Caesar to Rome, but returned home after his assassination. She then became the mistress of Mark Antony, who lived with her in Egypt. In 32, when Octavian drove Mark Antony's supporters out of Rome and declared war on Cleopatra, she sailed with her fleet to support her lover.

The end of the republic

The final showdown came in 31, at the Battle of Actium. Mark Antony and Cleopatra were defeated and fled back to Egypt, where they committed suicide the following year. Octavian was now undisputed ruler of Rome. He offered to return power to the Senate, but it was clear that only he could unite Rome. In 27, the Senate gave him a new name – Augustus, meaning 'deeply respected one' – and titled him imperator (supreme commander). The Roman empire had begun.

▲ The Battle of Actium was fought off the Adriatic coast of Greece on 2 September 31. Octavian's fleet of 400 warships easily outnumbered Antony and Cleopatra's fleet of 230 ships. After a brief skirmish, Cleopatra's squadron broke free and fled back to Egypt, followed by Mark Antony, leaving most of their fleet to be captured by Octavian.

◄ After the defeat of Mark Antony and Cleopatra, and their subsequent suicide, Egypt became part of the Roman empire. This special coin bearing the legend Aegypt Capta – 'Egypt captured' – was made by the victorious Octavian to commemorate the event.

SUMMARY OF CHAPTER 1: FROM CITY TO EMPIRE

Carthaginian terracotta head, c.6th–7th century BCE

Conquering Italy

From its foundation as a small village sometime during the 800s BCE, Rome grew slowly into a busy city occupying seven hills next to the River Tiber. Its first rulers were kings, but in 510 the last of the kings was expelled and the city became a republic. At this time, it was just one of many city-states in the region, competing for power with Sabines, Samnites, Etruscans and other tribes. But as these were gradually overcome, colonies of Romans settled throughout Latium (central Italy) and beyond.

However, there was nothing inevitable about Rome's expansion. Several times the city was almost overwhelmed, notably when the Gauls invaded and occupied it in 390.

But the Romans were good fighters and had set up a stable political organization led by able leaders. Early disputes between patricians and plebeians had been settled, giving every citizen a say in how the republic was governed.

Conquering the world

By 264, Rome controlled the whole of the Italian peninsula. Three lengthy wars with mighty Carthage gave it control of North Africa, Spain and the western Mediterranean by 146. To its east, Rome defeated Macedonia in 168 and acquired the rest of Greece in 146. When the king of Pergamum died in 133, he gave his kingdom to Rome, its first province in Asia. Julius Caesar conquered Gaul (France) by 50 and twice invaded Britain.

This constant warfare led to conflict in Rome itself. From the 130s onwards, generals and politicians struggled for power. One such general, Julius Caesar, made himself dictator in 44 but he was assassinated, causing a period of civil war until his adopted son, Octavian, reunited the republic in 30. Three years later, and now known as Augustus, he became the first emperor of Rome.

Go further...

Find out more about the history of the Roman republic and empire, its cities, armies and people:
www.historylearningsite.co.uk/a_history_of_ancient_rome.htm

For more information on the Romans in Britain:
www.romans-in-britain.org.uk

Archaeology by Trevor Barnes (Kingfisher Knowledge, 2004)

Roman Britain: A Very Short Introduction by Peter Salway (Oxford University Press, 2000)

Eyewitness Ancient Rome by Simon James (Dorling Kindersley, 1990)

Archaeologist
Uncovers the material remains of Roman and other civilizations.

Historian
Studies the written history and literature of ancient Rome.

Prop and costume maker
Creates historical costumes and artefacts for Roman military re-enactments.

Teacher
Passes on knowledge and enthusiasm about Rome to future generations.

Website designer
Creates sites dedicated to ancient Rome.

Visit the British Museum to see ancient Etruscan, British, Roman, Egyptian and other ancient artefacts:
The British Museum,
Great Russell Street,
London WC1B 3BG
Telephone: +44 (0) 20 7323 8482
www.thebritishmuseum.ac.uk

See the headquarters of the Second Augustan Legion in Britain at Caerleon outside Newport, South Wales, and the nearby Roman baths:
Roman Legionary Museum,
High Street,
Caerleon,
Gwent NP6 1AE
Telephone: +44 (0) 1633 423134
www.nmgw.ac.uk

Forum Romanum, Rome

CHAPTER 2

Life in imperial Rome

At the height of its power in the early 2nd century CE, the Roman empire was the greatest and grandest civilization in the world. Its towns and cities were packed with fine houses, shops and workplaces, luxurious public baths, amphitheatres and temples, while the countryside was extensively farmed to provide food, drink and other produce for everyone. The Romans were great engineers, building an excellent road network to connect the far-flung parts of the empire with the imperial capital, and aqueducts to bring water into the great cities. Their empire was well-defended with frontier forts and walls, while peace and order reigned within. At the heart of this empire was the capital city of Rome, at the time the finest and largest city in the world, ruled over by a series of powerful emperors. So mighty was this empire that it appeared it would last for ever.

Hadrian's Wall

Britain

**Germania
(Germany)**

Roman limites

► The Roman empire was mainly contained within natural borders: the Sahara and Arabian deserts to its south, the Atlantic Ocean to its west, and the Rhine and Danube rivers to its north. Only in the north of Britain, parts of Germany and western Asia did it have to defend long land borders.

Gaul (France)

Atlantic Ocean

Amphitheatre
at Nimes

Italy

Colosseum in Rome

Spain

Aqueduct at Segovia

Sardinia

Pompeii

Greece

Ruins at
Carthage

Sicily

Africa

The Roman empire

From the reign of Augustus onwards, the Roman empire steadily expanded until, in CE117, it reached its greatest extent. By then, it stretched 4,000km from west to east, and was home to more than 50 million people.

Securing the frontiers

Under the first emperor Augustus (see pages 22–23), the northern frontier of the empire was secured along the Danube river with the conquest of the Alps and the northern Balkans. An attempt to move the north-eastern frontier from the Rhine up to the Elbe was largely abandoned after a heavy defeat by Germanic tribes in CE9.

► In CE60, Queen Boudicca of the eastern Iceni tribe led the last serious opposition to Roman rule in Britain. She captured and burned the garrison towns of Colchester, St Albans and London, and was only defeated a year later, in a pitched battle somewhere in the Midlands.

► The Roman legions built their own boats. When they had to cross a major river, they tied them together to form a pontoon bridge. In this way they were able to outwit and defeat their many opponents.

Dacia
(Romania)

Black Sea

Constantinople

Asia Minor
(Turkey)

Armenia

Syria

Mediterranean Sea

Mesopotamia (Iraq)

Palmyra

Parthian empire
(Iran)

Egypt

West and east

In 43, Emperor Claudius (ruled 41–54) conquered Britain in an attempt to increase his own prestige in Rome. Later, Emperor Trajan (ruled 98–117) expanded the empire north into Dacia (Romania) by 106 and, after a rapid campaign against the Parthians, east into Armenia, Mesopotamia (Iraq) and on to the Persian Gulf by 117.

Revolt and repression

This constant conquest and expansion made the vast empire difficult to control. In Britain, the Iceni tribe was the first of many to rise in revolt in 47, while rebellions broke out against Emperor Nero (ruled 54–68) in both Gaul (France) and Spain. One of the most serious revolts broke out in Judea, when the Jews seized the capital, Jerusalem, in 66 and held it until it was recaptured in 70. The Jewish revolt was finally suppressed at the fortress of Masada in 74, when its defenders committed suicide rather than submit to Roman rule.

Roman roads

'All roads lead to Rome' is a saying that was certainly true in the Roman empire. Before the Romans, there were few paved roads in Europe, although there were many winding tracks and paths. When the Romans came along, they constructed an impressive system of straight roads that connected the entire empire to the imperial capital.

From A to B

The main requirement of a Roman road was that it be as straight and flat as possible so that legionaries could march quickly along it for hours at a time. The soldiers needed to move from one military fort or base to another in order to keep the peace. These forts were often situated in existing towns, or later had towns grow up around them, so travellers and traders also journeyed along these roads.

▼ The Romans built their roads in as straight a line as possible, climbing up and down hillsides and across valleys and moors, only changing direction to avoid a large river bend, a steep hill or other natural obstacle. The surface was smooth to allow foot soldiers to march along it in comfort and at speed.

▲ Roman roads were packed with every kind of traveller, from these magistrates (2nd-century CE relief) – elected government officials – walking in procession, to legions, merchants, tourists and robbers.

By aligning two of the hanging plumb lines on a groma, a surveyor made sure the road was straight.

A caravan used by travellers.

Getting it straight

The first task when building a road was to plot the route. We are not quite sure how the Romans did this, but they probably used a system of marker points on hills and other prominent natural features – perhaps involving beacons or bonfires – to mark out the entire route in outline. This is why most Roman roads are not completely straight, but made up of straight sections linked together in a series of very gentle zigzags. Once the overall route was planned, surveyors marked it out in detail using a groma (a sighting instrument).

Paved and drained

The road surface varied according to the local materials available. Most roads had a foundation of large stones covered by a layer of smaller stones and then a layer of gravel, on top of which were sometimes placed large paving stones. The road was up to 1m thick and up to 9m wide, sloping down to either side to let rainwater flow off into drainage ditches. When the surface wore out, a new one was placed on top. How many kilometres of roads the Romans built like this is unknown, but there were at least 16,000km in Britain alone.

▲ It is likely the Romans drew maps to help them on their travels (13th-century CE copy of an ancient map, above). Like modern-day maps, they show the various towns and cities and the distances between them, and even use symbols to show the inns and other stopping places along the route.

Most roads were built by legionaries using local slave labour when necessary.

The ditches on either side of the road drained away water.

Stone milestones or pillars marked every Roman mile (about 1.48km) of road.

Roman fortifications

When Hadrian (ruled CE117–138) became emperor after the death of Trajan (see page 27), he decided to end the expansion of the empire and instead secure it within its existing borders. Along the more dangerous of these borders he built a series of fortified barriers. The most famous is the wall named after him in northern England, but the most remarkable were the fortified limites he built in Germany.

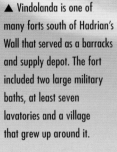

▲ Vindolanda is one of many forts south of Hadrian's Wall that served as a barracks and supply depot. The fort included two large military baths, at least seven lavatories and a village that grew up around it.

The weakest link

The boundary of the Roman empire mainly followed natural features, such as deserts, oceans, rivers and lakes, but the empire was always vulnerable to attack where its frontier crossed land. One of its weakest points was the land gap between the Rhine and Danube rivers, southeast of what is now Bonn in southern Germany.

Wooden palisade defended the military road from attack

Lines of cut-off or broken brushwood, often with thorns

Sharpened stakes with metal tips sunk into pits in the ground

The wooden wall

Ever since the reign of Claudius (see page 27), the frontier along the upper reaches of the Rhine and Danube rivers in central Europe had been fortified by limites, a line of forts linked by roads forming a militarized frontier zone. These ran along the empire's side of the riverbank or across hilltops and other easily secured places. Hadrian decided to strengthen this defence by building a substantial wooden palisade (fence) along 450km of its weakest point. This massive fortification consisted of wooden watchtowers, later replaced by stone structures, connected by a well-defended wooden track sitting on top of a huge earthen wall. Garrisons of defending soldiers were housed in barracks some 2km to the rear.

The obstacle course

Stretching in front of this wall for up to 150m were lines of dry ditches, water-filled moats, brushwood barriers, 30cm-long sharpened stakes with metal points and other defences. Some of these stakes were concealed in sunken pits. Together, these defences formed a massive obstacle course through which any enemy force would have to pass before it could reach the wall. No wonder the Roman empire remained so strong and secure for such a long time.

▲ Hadrian's Wall (remains, above) stretched 117km across the narrowest part of northern England from the Solway Firth east to the River Tyne. The wall was built mainly of stone – turf at the western end – and was 3m wide and up to 6m high. Along its length was a series of mile-castles, with two turrets or watchtowers in between to allow speedy signal communication along its length.

Wooden stakes driven into the earth made scaling the wall very difficult

Water-filled ditch

◄ The Roman limites, which were similar to this fortification, were built between the Rhine and Danube rivers in southern Germany. They ran across valleys and exposed tops of hills where no natural defences, such as rivers or steep gorges, existed. These formidable defences lasted for more than 300 years before they were overwhelmed and abandoned during the 5th century CE.

▲ Although the Forum today is largely in ruins, many paintings reveal the previous grandeur of its buildings. It was dotted with statues of emperors, triumphal arches and temples to the gods, as well as numerous public buildings.

Imperial Rome

The imperial city of Rome was by far the grandest and most important city in the whole of Europe. Here, the emperor lived in magnificent splendour, and in its beautiful buildings his government made the important decisions that affected the lives of all his people across the empire. But Rome had not always been so grand.

Cleaning up the city

When Augustus became emperor in 27BCE, Rome was a packed, dirty city in which one million people lived and worked and struggled to earn a living. Its streets were shabby and crowded and many of its public buildings were nondescript and dull. The River Tiber was so filled with rubbish and hemmed in by houses that it often flooded. Augustus changed all this. He re-organized the city into 14 districts, each with its own administration, and set up a police and a fire service. He dredged and widened the river, built and restored several aqueducts (see pages 34–35), and demolished many narrow streets.

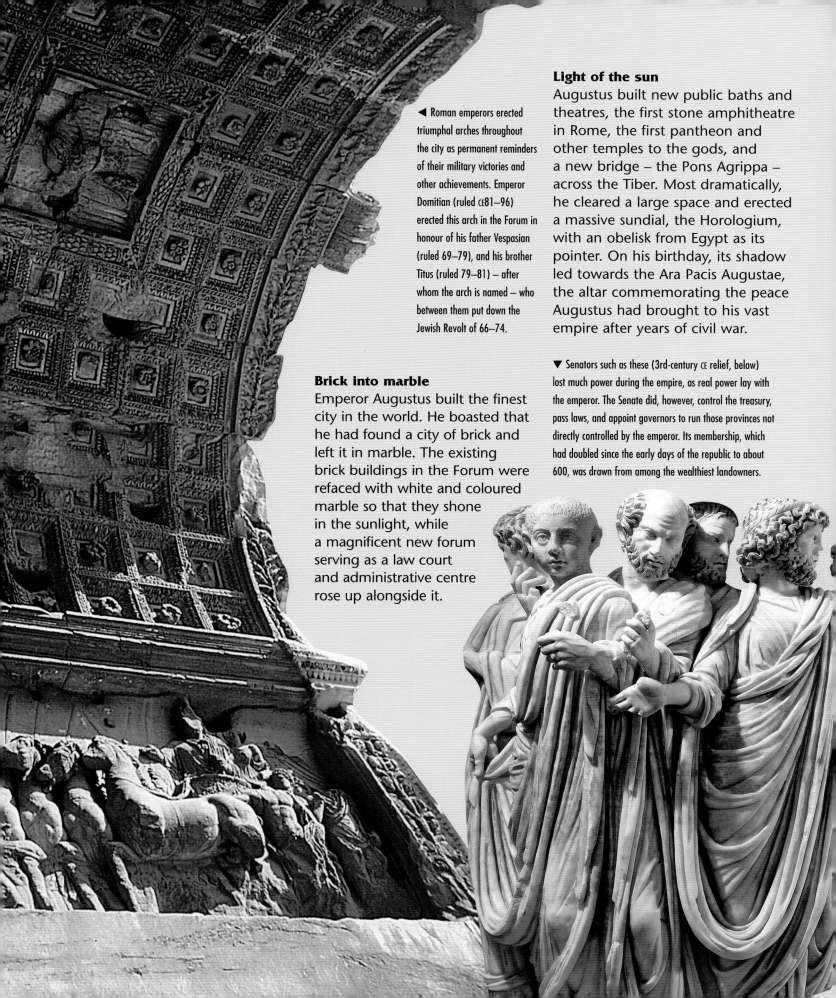

◄ Roman emperors erected triumphal arches throughout the city as permanent reminders of their military victories and other achievements. Emperor Domitian (ruled CE 81–96) erected this arch in the Forum in honour of his father Vespasian (ruled 69–79), and his brother Titus (ruled 79–81) – after whom the arch is named – who between them put down the Jewish Revolt of 66–74.

Light of the sun

Augustus built new public baths and theatres, the first stone amphitheatre in Rome, the first pantheon and other temples to the gods, and a new bridge – the Pons Agrippa – across the Tiber. Most dramatically, he cleared a large space and erected a massive sundial, the Horologium, with an obelisk from Egypt as its pointer. On his birthday, its shadow led towards the Ara Pacis Augustae, the altar commemorating the peace Augustus had brought to his vast empire after years of civil war.

Brick into marble

Emperor Augustus built the finest city in the world. He boasted that he had found a city of brick and left it in marble. The existing brick buildings in the Forum were refaced with white and coloured marble so that they shone in the sunlight, while a magnificent new forum serving as a law court and administrative centre rose up alongside it.

▼ Senators such as these (3rd-century CE relief, below) lost much power during the empire, as real power lay with the emperor. The Senate did, however, control the treasury, pass laws, and appoint governors to run those provinces not directly controlled by the emperor. Its membership, which had doubled since the early days of the republic to about 600, was drawn from among the wealthiest landowners.

▲ Underground cisterns were used to store water in many of the great Roman cities. These cisterns, which looked rather like flooded cellars, were usually built of stone, although some were carved out of solid rock. Water flowed into the cisterns through aqueducts and underground pipes.

Bringing water

The Romans were master engineers, constructing everything from paved roads (see pages 28–29) and arched bridges to underfloor heating systems and simple fire engines. But one of their greatest achievements was the one we probably all take for granted today: a ready supply of fresh, running water. Indeed, so great was their achievement that it was not properly surpassed until the 19th century CE, when most industrial towns and cities were first supplied with running water. For the Romans, water was a necessity, not a luxury, as large parts of the empire had a hot climate where water was in short supply.

▲ Communal public lavatories – without any partitions – were common in Roman towns. These consisted of a row or semicircle of stone seats, sometimes with wooden seats. Dirty water from the public baths flowed under the seats to flush away the waste into underground sewers beneath the streets. A gutter of running water ran in front for washing.

▼ Sextus Julius Frontinus (c.CE30–104) was a former consul who served as administrator of the water supply to Rome around 97. He got to know Rome's system of aqueducts so well that he wrote a two-volume study – *De Aquis Urbis Romae* (On the Water Supply of Rome) – about the history of aqueducts, their technical details and how they should be constructed.

Aqueduct supply

Many Roman towns were built near rivers or springs, ensuring a flow of fresh water. But where water was scarce, or usage was high, it had to be brought in from a nearby source along an aqueduct. This consisted of a gently sloping conduit (pipe) running on or just below the surface, through which water flowed under gravity into a large storage reservoir.

▼ Water flowed into Rome though a series of overground and underground aqueducts, one of which can be seen snaking through the bottom left of the city below. Where it crossed between two hills, the aqueduct ran along the top of an arched viaduct.

Watering the people

Once in the reservoir, the water passed through a series of tanks to remove any impurities. It then flowed into the main city distribution tank and on through lead pipes into the many public baths and fountains, from which people fetched their own water. Private houses often had their own water supply, as well as a system for collecting rainwater from the roof.

Cleaning the people

Every Roman town had its own public baths. Underground furnaces pumped hot air into the hypocaust, a system of brick pillars supporting the floor that allowed hot air to flow through it and into the wall cavities. So the baths provided a series of hot pools, steam rooms and saunas, as well as cold plunge baths in which to cool down.

Life in the city

When we think of Rome, or any Roman city, we usually think of grand public buildings and statues and large ceremonial arches. We assume that most Romans lived in luxury in beautiful villas and other large houses, with slaves to look after them and wonderful food to eat. The reality, however, was quite different, for alongside this grand vision was the real city, one of noise and dirt and slums. Most Romans lived squashed together in squalid, overcrowded apartment blocks.

▼ Trajan's Market was built during the reign of Emperor Trajan (see page 27) as a purpose-built shopping centre of 150 shops, offices and apartments. The left-hand side of this photograph shows what it might have looked like when it was first constructed.

High-rise blocks
These apartment blocks were usually three or four storeys high, with shops, workshops and bars at street level and then floors of small flats or even single rooms above. Most blocks were built quickly and badly using poor materials, so they often collapsed. Everyone shared the same lavatory, and the water supply did not reach above the first floor.

▼ Most of the shopkeepers who worked in the market were men, although records of the period do list three female wool-sellers, two women jewellers, a greengrocer and a fishwife.

Fear of fire

Most apartments had no heating system, so the occupants burned wood logs in open metal braziers for heat, hot water and cooking. As a result, fires were common. Indeed, they got so bad that Emperor Augustus (see pages 32–33) set up teams of vigiles (firefighting slaves) equipped with buckets of water and simple wooden water pumps to tackle the many blazes.

Night life

During the day, Rome's narrow streets bustled with activity. Carts were banned, so shopkeepers could display their goods to passing customers. While the main streets were swept clean, most were very dirty, as people just threw their rubbish out of the windows. At night, the city changed character completely. It was pitch black, as there were no streetlights, and thieves took to the streets. One wit, the poet Juvenal (CE60–130), even said that it was stupid to go out at night without first having made a will.

▶ Unlike an apartment, a Roman domus or house was quite spacious. It was arranged around an atrium or hall, where guests were received and members of the household could relax. The centre of the atrium was open and often contained an impluvium or pool, as well as a lararium or shrine to the household gods set into one of the walls.

▼ Shops selling vegetables, fruit and flowers occupied the ground floor, with larger shops selling wine and olive oil above them. Offices and apartments occupied the upper floors. Most shops opened early in the morning and closed before noon, so it was important to get up early if you wanted food to eat.

Life in the country

Many Romans did not live in towns or cities, but in small villages and isolated hamlets in the countryside. There, they were joined by affluent city people who owned villas outside town. The countryside was, however, not just a place to relax, but a vast rural industry, producing all the food, drink, wool and other products needed to keep the Roman empire fed, watered and clothed.

▶ Pomona (18th-century CE sculpture, right) was the Roman goddess of poma, or tree fruits such as apples and pears. She is often linked with Vertumnus (far right), the god of autumn and the changing seasons.

▼ Country villas were often very luxurious affairs, with lavish paintings on the walls and intricate mosaics on the floors. The rooms were arranged around a central courtyard garden, and often had underfloor central heating. Most villas had hot and cold baths and even a swimming pool.

Shady cloister

Swimming pool

Central courtyard with fountain

The big estate

The first farms in the Roman republic were small, producing enough food to feed the family with a little left to sell in the market. But during the Carthaginian wars (see pages 16–17), many farmers fought in the army and left their farms for good. Rich landowners bought up these empty farms and merged them into latifundia (vast country estates), creating huge profits and wealth for their owners.

Food for the cities

Roman farms produced everything a city-dweller needed to survive: olive oil, wine, fruit and vegetables, grain for bread, fresh meat and fish, milk, cheese, wool, building materials, and wood to burn for heating and making furniture. Some of these goods just went to the local markets, but wine and olive oil were exported all over the empire: most of Rome's grain came from Egypt.

Slave labour

The main labour force on these huge estates were slaves (see page 40), who worked long hours for just their food and lodging. They had to plant and reap the cereal harvest of wheat, oats or barley, look after the vegetable plots, the grape vines and fruit orchards, feed the goats and pigs, tend the sheep on the higher, less fertile pastures, and do all the menial jobs such as mending fences.

Dining hall

Kitchen

Bedroom

Domestic life

The centre of Roman life was the family, headed by the powerful paterfamilias (father) who had authority over everyone in the house. Women were respected as wives, but had few rights of their own, while children were bought up to serve the empire and improve the family's status. Boys trained for a life in the army or government while girls were expected to marry.

▲ Roman children wrote their lessons on a wax tablet using a stylus, a type of pen, to scratch words into the wax. The stylus was made of iron, bronze or bone and had a pointed end for writing and a flat end for rubbing out. Children also wrote their lessons using pen, ink and parchment paper.

Slaves

Rich Romans owned slaves to work in their homes, businesses and farms. Many slaves lived in terrible conditions, working long hours in mines, building sites and other dangerous places. A few became gladiators (see pages 42–43). Some became members of the family and their children were brought up with the master's children. Educated slaves worked as tutors, doctors and in other professional jobs, including government posts.

Education

Only children from fairly rich families went to school, as the richest children had private tutors at home while the poorest had no formal education. From the ages of seven to 11, boys, and some girls, learned reading, writing and arithmetic at the local ludus (primary school). A few boys then went on to the grammaticus (secondary school); girls stayed at home to learn household skills.

Baker selling bread

Pharmacist preparing medicines

Butcher chopping meat

▲ Slaves were bought and sold by local dealers. Most were prisoners-of-war captured when Rome conquered their homeland, or were the children of existing slaves, although a few were the children of poor people, sold to pay off family debts. Slaves could be freed by their masters or could save up to buy their freedom as freedmen and women.

Women

Most Roman women married in their early teens but kept the right to inherit, own and sell off property. They were in charge of the family home and its finances, and looked after their children until they began school, although they had no legal rights over them. Outside the home, they were excluded from political and public life, apart from the very few who became priestesses.

▲ Rich women had many slaves to look after them and do all the menial work about the house. Poorer women, however, did this work themselves, as well as working in the family business or farm, or as midwives, hairdressers and in other traditional women's jobs.

▼ The Romans did not have department stores or supermarkets selling a wide range of goods. Instead, each shop specialized in a different product or service, just like the old-fashioned high street shops used to do. These shops were family-run businesses, often relying on slave labour for the more laborious tasks.

Grocer in his shop

Tavern landlord

The Colosseum

On public holidays and other special occasions, Roman citizens poured into the local amphitheatre to enjoy a good day's sport. Every major town and city had its own amphitheatre, which looked much like a modern football stadium. Here, professional gladiators fought each other with swords and tridents, sometimes to the death.

Rome's Colosseum

The biggest amphitheatre in the Roman empire was the Colosseum in Rome. It opened in CE80 with a gladiatorial festival lasting 100 days and then staged games 93 times every year. Games lasted all day, starting in the morning with a parade of gladiators, musicians, dancers and jugglers. Then came the wild animals, including lions, tigers, bears and even crocodiles, which performed tricks or fought each other. Armed hunters then fought the beasts, while unarmed criminals were thrown into the ring to be torn to pieces in front of the crowd.

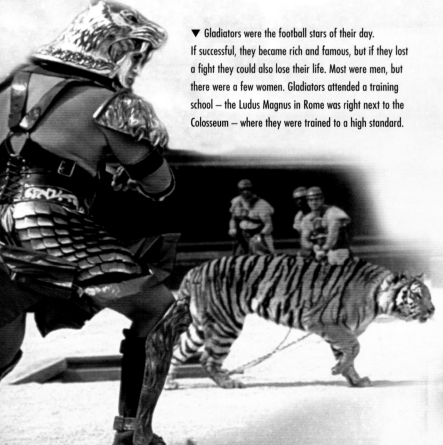

▼ Gladiators were the football stars of their day. If successful, they became rich and famous, but if they lost a fight they could also lose their life. Most were men, but there were a few women. Gladiators attended a training school – the Ludus Magnus in Rome was right next to the Colosseum – where they were trained to a high standard.

Gladiators

After the arena was cleared and the blood soaked up with new sand, the gladiators entered the ring. Gladiators were usually prisoners-of-war, criminals or slaves, although a few were volunteers. Many different types of gladiator fought each other during the games, each with different weapons and costumes. For instance, the lightly clothed retiarius used a weighted net and trident to ensnare his opponent, the secutor, whose special egg-shaped helmet was designed to avoid snagging in the net.

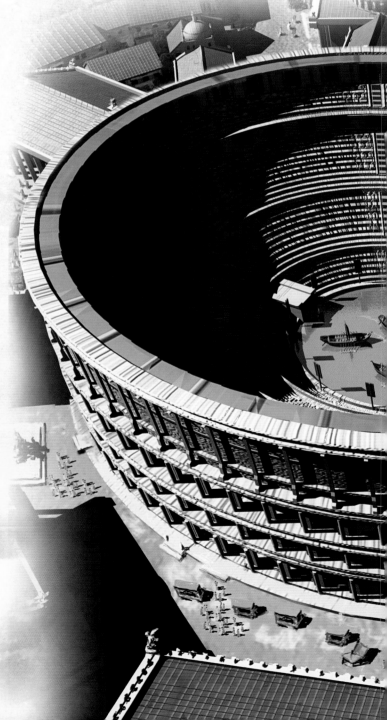

▼ The floor of the Colosseum was very occasionally flooded so that mock sea battles could be waged between gladiators rowing small warships. It was very popular, so several arenas were built for this specific purpose in Rome.

▶ Although partially ruined, it is still possible to see how splendid the Colosseum must have been. At 188m long, 156m wide and 40m high, its five tiers of seating held more than 50,000 people, who entered through 76 different entrances. Women sat alone on a special terrace near the top. When the weather was hot, a massive awning was pulled over the top to protect spectators from the sun. Wild animals kept in cages below the arena entered through a series of trapdoors in the floor, while gladiators had their own tunnel.

Death or glory

If a gladiator was badly wounded, he could appeal to the referee or even the emperor, sitting on a throne in his ringside box, to stop the fight. After the audience had made their views known with cheers or boos, the emperor made his decision whether or not to let the gladiator live. Most were spared, as gladiator training was too expensive to lose too many gladiators! The victor was given a crown and money, and over the years could become rich and famous. After many victories, he was given a wooden sword, a sign that his fighting days were over and he was a free man.

A day at the races

Even more than cheering on their favourite gladiator, the Romans loved a day out at the chariot races. The thrill of watching horse-drawn chariots race brought hundreds of thousands of people to every event. For this was family entertainment on a grand scale, although sometimes passions got out of hand and riots erupted when a favourite team lost!

▲ The chariots raced seven times around the Circus Maximus in a counter-clockwise direction, a total of about 8km. At the end of each lap, a large golden marker in the shape of a dolphin — some sources say an egg — was turned over to show how many laps were left. The race finished in front of the emperor's box.

▶ The lightweight chariots were usually pulled by two or four horses, but sometimes six or eight horses, camels or elephants were used, adding to the excitement. To stop himself falling off, the charioteer wrapped the reins around him. He also carried a dagger, so that he could cut himself free if his chariot overturned.

Circus Maximus

Every Roman town and city had its own racetrack, but by far the largest was the one in Rome. The Circus Maximus could accommodate 250,000 people, more than any sports stadium in the world today. Unlike at the Colosseum, men and women sat together, so families started arriving at the racetrack early in the morning to get a good seat. They bought food and drink from vendors at the track, placed bets on their favourite team, and settled down to enjoy a good day's sport. A local magistrate ran the races, although sometimes the emperor himself officiated. When a trumpet sounded, the official raised a white cloth. When he dropped the cloth, the starting gates opened and up to 12 chariots flew out to begin the first race.

Thrills and spills

As many as 24 races were held each day. Charioteers were usually slaves, although some were highly paid professionals, and raced in teams – the four teams in Rome were the Reds, Whites, Blues and Greens, all owned by the emperor. The most dangerous part of the race was turning the tight corner at each end of the track. Crashes were common and both charioteer and horses were often injured. The winner received the victor's palm leaf, a gold necklace and money – and lived to race another day!

Roman theatre

As well as blood sports and chariot racing, the Romans went to the theatre (a fresco from Pompeii of a theatre mask, right). Just like today, Roman audiences enjoyed tragedies, comedies, pantomimes and mimes, some of which were very rude or very violent. Acting was not a respectable profession, so most actors were either slaves or freedmen. Successful actors were treated just like Oscar-winners today, and some became so popular that women were not allowed to sit in the front rows of the audience in case they tried to run off with one of the stars!

▼ The Circus Maximus in Rome was 570m long and 140m wide, with stands up to 28m high. The starting gates were at the left end of the track, the emperor's box mid-way down the right-hand side. Trophies, statues, an obelisk from Egypt and the lap counter stood on the spina (the central barrier).

Roman religion

The first Romans were farmers and they worshipped the numina (spirits) that lived around them in each stream, field and wood. To keep these nature gods happy and to ensure good weather or a plentiful harvest, people made sacrifices and offerings to the gods at local shrines. This practice continued throughout the republic and empire, as Romans continued to worship their own household and local gods and offer them simple presents in return for protection.

▲ The Romans frequently adopted Greek gods and gave them Latin names. Zeus (above), the supreme Greek god, was renamed Jupiter; Eros, the god of love, became Cupid; and Ares, the god of war, became Mars.

State gods

Over the centuries, the Romans also developed a state religion based around three powerful gods: Jupiter, the sky god; Juno, his wife and goddess of women; and Minerva, their daughter and goddess of wisdom. These three were joined by many others, mainly 'borrowed' from Greece. Each god or goddess looked after a different aspect of daily life. Like the Greeks, the Romans gave their gods human form, built temples in their honour, and worshipped them at festivals, when they made offerings to obtain the god's blessing.

◀ The Persian god Mithras was one of the many foreign gods imported into Roman worship. Only men could worship him, which was why he was very popular in the army. His followers met in underground temples and endured secret, often terrifying rituals. Here, he is shown slaying a bull, whose blood gave life to the Universe according to legend.

The divine emperors

After the death of the first emperor, Augustus, his successor Tiberius (ruled CE14–37) declared him a god. The mad emperor Caligula (ruled 37–41) actually believed he was a god and dressed up as Jupiter to impress and frighten his subjects. Across the empire, statues were erected to the imperial gods, although praying to the dead emperors was really much the same as showing respect to the Roman empire itself.

◀ Each household had its own lararium (shrine) dedicated to the family gods. Here, the family prayed daily and placed offerings of food and wine in front of the statuettes representing their gods.

▶ The six Vestal Virgins were the only priestesses in Rome. Their job was to tend the eternal flame of the goddess Vesta, as Romans believed that their city would remain strong only while the flame burned.

▶ Until c.ce313, Christians were frequently persecuted for their beliefs. Many were imprisoned, tortured or killed during the persecution ordered by Nero, while hundreds were literally thrown to the lions in public amphitheatres.

The coming of Christianity

The Romans were very good at absorbing gods and beliefs from other countries and were tolerant of those with a different faith. The exception were Jews and Christians, whom the Romans persecuted for refusing to worship the emperor. Emperor Nero (ruled 54–68) blamed Christians for starting the fire that almost destroyed Rome in 64. For the next 200 years Christians were forced to worship in secret for fear of persecution.

Pompeii

On the morning of 24 August CE79, the people of Pompeii, a Roman town south of Rome on the Bay of Naples, woke to a summer's day like any other. But as the day wore on, the sky grew dark. Suddenly the long-dormant volcano of Mount Vesuvius exploded, showering Pompeii with hot ash and rock. As people tried to escape, coughing and spluttering through the hot, dark, swirling clouds, they and the people of neighbouring Herculaneum were gradually overwhelmed by a lethal blast of gas and ash. Within hours, both towns and their inhabitants were buried several metres deep.

Dead and buried

Pompeii and Herculaneum remained buried for the next 1,700 years, a forgotten time capsule from the Roman empire. During the 18th century CE, archaeologists began to excavate both sites, hoping they might uncover some interesting remains. What they found, however, was beyond their wildest dreams, for here were two perfectly preserved Roman towns that have since told us more about what it was like to live and work in the Roman empire than almost anywhere else.

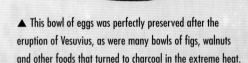

▲ This bowl of eggs was perfectly preserved after the eruption of Vesuvius, as were many bowls of figs, walnuts and other foods that turned to charcoal in the extreme heat.

▼ It is almost impossible to imagine the terror experienced by the people of Pompeii and Herculaneum when the clouds of ash and gas suffocated all those who had not managed to escape.

Living in style

Pompeii was a rich and bustling port, exporting wine, olive oil and wool. Some people lived in beautiful houses, many of them built around a central courtyard, that were decorated with colourful wall paintings and filled with fine furniture, statues and other items. The layers of ash preserved these houses perfectly, as well as preserving market stalls, baths, a theatre, an amphitheatre and a paelestra (gymnasium).

How the people lived

The ash also turned organic matter such as foodstuffs and wood into carbon, so we now know what Roman bread looked like from the solid carbon loaves found in a baker's brick oven, as well as other foods the inhabitants ate. All these finds give us an excellent idea of what a Roman town looked like and how its people lived their daily lives.

▲ The plaster casts of bodies gives us some idea of how the citizens of Pompeii died, huddled up together in terror as they tried to hide behind walls from the lethal blasts of gas and ash.

Entombed

The most disturbing discovery, however, were the remains of approximately 2,000 Pompeiians killed by the eruption. Dying where they fell, their bodies were covered in a tomb of ash that gradually solidified around them. Over the years, all but their bones decayed, leaving a hollow cast of their bodies in the solid rock. Archaeologists have either removed these bones or filled the body cast with plaster of Paris: when the plaster hardened, its case of rock was removed, leaving a perfect representation of an ancient Roman at the moment of death.

SUMMARY OF CHAPTER 2: LIFE IN IMPERIAL ROME

Creating the empire

After the accession of Augustus, the first emperor, in 27BCE, the Roman empire expanded considerably, adding new provinces in North Africa, Britain, the Rhine and Danube valleys and western Asia. This expansion was not always peaceful, however, as major revolts broke out in Britain, Judea and elsewhere, although all were put down with great severity. By the time of Emperor Trajan's death in CE117, the empire had reached its greatest extent. His successor, Hadrian, stopped the expansion and abandoned some territory in order to withdraw behind more secure frontiers. Major walls and lines of fortifications were built along land frontiers in Britain, Germany and Syria to defend the empire from possible attack.

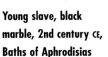

Young slave, black marble, 2nd century CE, Baths of Aphrodisias

Life in the empire

As the empire grew, Roman civilization spread out from Italy across the whole of the Mediterranean and Europe. New purpose-built roads helped troops and traders move around quickly, as well as connecting the new Roman towns and cities together. Trade in goods such as olive oil, wine and grain flourished. Entertainments including gladiator fights and chariot racing became popular, as did Roman theatre and literature.

At the heart of this big, bustling empire was the imperial capital of Rome. Augustus boasted that he found a city of brick and left it of marble, as many old buildings were refaced while new ones were erected. Rome was a city of great contrasts, with fabulous public buildings alongside many slum houses, and where great wealth existed side by side with even greater poverty. Massive arenas were built, notably the Colosseum and the Circus Maximus, to entertain the masses, while baths and other public amenities were also constructed. Water flowed into Rome, and other cities, along spectacular aqueducts. But not every city was so grand as Rome, nor lasted so long. Pompeii was overwhelmed by a volcanic eruption in 79 and buried for centuries. Luckily, its survival under the ash has enabled us to discover vast amounts about this great empire.

Go further...

Visit Nova Romana, a virtual Roman town: www.click-site.com

See Roman wall paintings and other remains from Roman London in the Museum of London: www.museumoflondon.org.uk

Ancient Rome by Peter Connolly (Oxford University Press, 2001)

The Penguin Historical Atlas of Ancient Rome by Chris Scarre (Penguin, 1995)

Handbook to Life in Ancient Rome by Lesley Adkins and Roy A Adkins (Facts on File, 2004)

Archaeologist
Studies the remains of Roman forts, villas, houses, baths and other buildings.

Volunteer
Helps local archaeologists with their excavation and conservation work.

Surveyor
Maps Roman sites.

Illustrator or photographer
Documents Roman sites.

Computer graphic artist
Recreates Roman towns, buildings and events on screen.

Tour guide
Escorts visitors around remains.

Explore the vast complex of Roman baths and spas at Bath, southern England:
Pump Room,
Stall Street,
Bath BA1 1LZ
Telephone: +44 (0) 1225 477791
www.romanbaths.co.uk

Hadrian's Wall – an early 2nd-century CE Roman wall – runs through Cumbria, Northumberland and Tyne & Wear in northern England:
www.hadrians-wall.org

See the Temple of Mithras and other Roman remains in the City of London:
Temple Court,
11 Queen Victoria Street,
London EC4
www.museumoflondon.org.uk

CHAPTER 3

Bust of Emperor Constantine and other artefacts, Rome

The end of the empire

Despite its apparent strength, the Roman empire suffered from some serious weaknesses. Its emperors were not always up to the job, while its long frontiers were difficult to defend against warlike neighbours. As a result, from the middle of the 2nd century CE onwards, the empire slowly began to weaken. Waves of barbarians swept in from the east, ravaging the countryside and even raiding Rome itself. To make it easier to govern, the capital was moved from Rome to the new city of Constantinople on the borders of Europe and Asia, and the empire itself was divided into eastern and western halves. By this time, Christianity was tolerated throughout the empire and the pagan temples had closed. The end of the empire came in 476, when the last Roman emperor in the west was overthrown. Yet the Roman empire still lives on, affecting our lives some 1,500 years after its demise.

The Roman emperors

From 27BCE to CE476, Rome was ruled by a series of emperors. Some, like the first emperor Augustus, were outstanding leaders who ruled wisely and fairly. Others, such as Caligula and Nero, were mad, bad and more than dangerous to know.

◄ Augustus was the adopted son of Julius Caesar (see pages 20–21) and the first Roman emperor, ruling from 27BCE to CE14. All subsequent emperors bore the title Augustus.

◄ The third emperor (ruled CE37–41) was given the nickname Caligula ('little boot') because of the miniature soldier's uniform he wore as a child. Seriously unwell after his accession, he soon became mentally ill, even trying to make his horse a consul. Caligula was assassinated at the Palatine Games in Rome to stop his endless cruelty.

◄ Roman emperors did not wear crowns, as they did not want to be thought of as kings. Instead they wore wreaths of laurel leaves, which were often used to reward victorious Roman generals.

▲ Most famous for playing the fiddle while Rome burned, Nero (ruled CE54–68) was accused of starting the great fire of Rome in 64 so that he could build a new palace. A good emperor at first, he later became tyrannical and killed both his wife and mother before committing suicide.

Division and dissent
The assassination by mutinous troops in 235 of the last Severan emperor, Severus Alexander (ruled 222–235), plunged the empire into a lengthy period of military anarchy and division, with separate emperors ruling both a western Gallic empire and an eastern empire based on the trading city of Palmyra in Syria. Unity was eventually restored as first Diocletian (ruled 284–305) and then Constantine I tackled the leadership and administrative problems of the empire.

◄ Under Trajan (ruled CE98–117) the Roman empire reached its greatest extent. He was a fine military commander whose exploits are commemorated on Trajan's Column in Rome.

▼ Commodus (ruled CE180–192) was another emperor who went mad in office. He tried to rename Rome 'colonia Commodiana' (colony of Commodus) and was assassinated shortly afterwards.

▲ In CE330, Constantine I (ruled 307–337) moved the imperial capital from Rome to Byzantium, which he renamed Constantinople. It remained capital of the eastern Roman or Byzantine empire until 1453.

The year of the five emperors
At first the emperors followed each other in hereditary succession, but in CE68, the incompetent and mad Nero committed suicide after rebellion broke out against his rule. Three military men and administrators followed him as emperor in quick succession until the military commander Vespasian (ruled 69–79) eventually took control the next year. There then followed a series of strong and competent emperors.

The year of the six emperors
The 2nd century CE was a period of relative stability until Commodus, another mad emperor, was assassinated in 192. This time five emperors struggled for power until Septimius Severus (ruled 193–211), a military commander, established the Severan dynasty. Rome was rebuilt and the empire's boundaries extended into Asia at the expense of the Parthian (Persian) empire.

Decline and fall of the Roman empire

Although the Roman empire appeared invincible, its very size and complexity made it difficult to govern, while its long land borders in Europe and Asia were always vulnerable to attack. Various emperors tried to make the empire more manageable, but during the 5th century CE enemy tribes poured across its borders, finally bringing the western empire to an end in 476.

Diocletian's reforms

When Diocletian (ruled CE284–305) became emperor, he realised that the empire was too big and complex for one man to rule alone. In 285, he named Maximian (250–310) as Caesar (junior emperor) to govern the western provinces while he ruled the east. A year later he promoted Maximian to become Augustus (senior emperor) alongside him. In 293, the pair each appointed a caesar to support them. Together, the four men restructured the empire by dividing up the provinces into smaller areas, and increased the size and efficiency of the army. The empire became so peaceful that Diocletian voluntarily retired to Croatia.

▲ In CE410, Visigoths under Alaric sacked Rome. Although no longer capital of the empire — Constantinople was capital of the eastern half, while the more easily defended Ravenna was capital of the west — the attacks sent shockwaves throughout the entire Roman world. The city was sacked again by the Vandals in 455 and never again reclaimed its grandeur or importance.

◀ For 650 years, the only defence Rome had was the Servian Wall, built during the 380s BCE. In CE271, as a sign of more troubled times, Emperor Aurelian (ruled 270–275) ordered the construction of a new and much stronger wall to surround the city, including the Porta Appia (now San Sebastiano, left) gate. The walls and gates were further strengthened in the early 300s and then again in 403 after the Goths invaded Italy.

◄ The four-man government of the empire set up by Diocletian was known as the tetrarchy. Its four members are shown in this porphyry (stone) sculpture. Although successful at first, the experiment did not last after Diocletian's abdication.

The last emperor

The Roman empire had been divided in two, but its western half was too weak to withstand these attacks. In 476, the last emperor, Romulus Augustus (ruled from 475), was overthrown and sent into retirement in a villa outside Naples. The empire in the west was at an end.

▼ Many Romans converted to Christianity as the religion gained official acceptance during the 4th century CE. They built or adapted small rooms in their villas to become private chapels. This painting of a Christian praying with outstretched arms is on the wall of one such chapel in Lullingstone villa in southern England, whose owner converted to Christianity sometime around CE360.

Constantine the Great

By 324, Constantine (ruled 307–337) reunited the empire under his sole rule. His predecessors had persecuted Christians because they refused to worship the Roman emperor: in 313, Constantine stopped the persecution of Christians. He also moved the imperial capital eastwards to the new city of Constantinople (now Istanbul) on the Bosphorus. From now on, the empire was split in two.

The end of the empire

From the 240s, the Goths – a Germanic tribe – raided the Balkan and Asian provinces. Other Germanic tribes raided western Europe. By the late 300s, the Visigoths came under pressure from the Huns to their east and poured into the Balkans. Alans, Vandals, Franks, Saxons and others swept into France, Spain and even Italy itself.

▲ Many planets – including Jupiter (above) and Mars – moons and stars are named after Roman gods.

▼ Both the French and American revolutionaries of the 18th century CE saw the Roman republic as an ideal model for their own new republics. The USA still has a senate and senators based on the Roman republican senate.

The Roman legacy

Although the Roman empire came to an end in CE476, its legacy has lived on right up to the present day, more than 1,500 years later. Politics, religion, the law, the calendar, language, architecture and much more have all been influenced by the Romans.

Politics

Throughout history, people have tried to recreate the Roman empire. In CE800, the Frankish king Charlemagne (742–814) was crowned 'Emperor of the Romans', controlling much of western Europe. In 962, Otto of Germany (ruled until 973) became the first Holy Roman emperor, ruling an empire based in Germany and Italy that lasted until 1806; its symbol was the Roman imperial eagle.

▲ The Vatican City in the heart of Rome is the headquarters of the Roman Catholic Church. St Peter, one of Christ's disciples and the first Bishop of Rome, is buried under the magnificent church that bears his name.

Religion and law

The Catholic Church established its headquarters in Rome when it was still the imperial capital. Today, the Bishop of Rome, known as the Pope, remains head of the Church. For centuries, Catholic priests and monks kept alive Roman learning, and until recently, all church services were held in Latin, the language of the Romans. Roman law still forms the basis of many European legal systems, while the Roman use of judge and jury to hear legal cases is almost universal today.

The calendar

The 365-day calendar – with an extra day every four years – introduced by Julius Caesar (see pages 20–21) and then fine-tuned in 1582 is still in use today. The Romans also gave us the 12-month year, the seven-day week and the names of our months.

▲ The most obvious political legacy of the Roman empire in existence today is the European Union, originally set up by the six western European nations that signed the 1957 Treaty of Rome. It now has 25 member states, from Portugal in the west to the Baltic States on the borders of Russia in the east. Although not a single state like the Roman empire, the EU aims to achieve European unity through co-operation and collaboration.

▶ We still use Roman numerals today on clocks and watches, sundials and to number our kings and queens.

◀ Scientists classify and name plants, such as this *passiflora mollissima* (passionflower), and animals in the international language of Latin to avoid any misunderstanding.

Towns and cities

The Romans borrowed much of their architectural style from the Greeks; we in turn have borrowed much from the Romans. Many of our great cities have public buildings modelled on earlier Roman examples, while many of our roads follow the old Roman roads. Our water and sewage systems owe much to the Romans, and like them we enjoy central heating, public baths and even fast food. Whether we are aware of it or not, the Romans are still with us today.

The Latin language

Modern-day languages such as Italian, French, Spanish, Portuguese and Romanian are all directly descended from Latin, while even the seemingly unrelated English includes thousands of Latin-based words and phrases. Although no longer spoken or written today, Latin is still used to classify and name plants and animals, and is still useful in medicine, the law and other professions. Of the 26 letters in our alphabet, 22 come from the Roman alphabet: the Romans had no W or Y, and used I for both I and J, and V for both U and V.

▶ This ruin is part of the remains of a city built by the Romans in Apamea, Syria, in the 2nd century CE. Pillars, colonnades and other features of Roman architecture which we call 'classical' in style are still used today in many modern buildings.

SUMMARY OF CHAPTER 3: THE END OF THE EMPIRE

Reorganization and division

The Roman empire faced two main problems: internally, how to govern such a large and sprawling territory, and externally, how to stop those who tried to flood into the empire in search of land and booty. The first problem was addressed by administrative changes under both Septimius Severan and Diocletian that split the empire into smaller divisions, preventing one provincial governor gaining too much power, and that strengthened the army. Diocletian tried to divide the rule of the empire between four people – the tetrarchy – but that system collapsed after his abdication. Eventually, Constantine moved the capital of the empire east. The empire was then formally split into eastern and western halves to make it more governable. These 4th-century reforms allowed the empire to recover some of its strength.

**The tetrarchy,
St Mark's Square,
Venice, Italy (c.CE305)**

Numerous tribes

The external problem was far more difficult to control. Numerous nomadic and warlike tribes from eastern Europe and central Asia looked enviously across the frontier at the fertile land and wealth of Rome. From the 240s onwards, they posed a problem first in the Balkans and Asia Minor, and then in Germany. The Romans strengthened their defences and gave up territory, but they were eventually overwhelmed by the sheer weight of numbers. In 375, the Visigoths crossed into Bulgaria and were allowed to settle there, but they soon rebelled and in 410 sacked Rome itself. More tribes then poured over the frontier and settled throughout western Europe. By the time the last western emperor was deposed in 476, the Roman empire existed in name only.

The end of the empire?

But the empire did not come to a complete end, as the tribal kingdoms of the west required Roman administrators to govern their new kingdoms. The eastern empire, under its capable emperors, even managed to recover some land in the west during the 6th century and survived until 1453.

Go further...

Look at some outstanding remains from across the Roman empire, as well as interactive maps and other information: www.roman-empire.net

Check which museums in your area have Roman artefacts: www.museums.co.uk

What the Romans Did For Us by Philip Wilkinson (Boxtree, 2000)

A Guide to the Roman Remains in Britain by Roger J A Wilson (Constable, 2002)

The Ruthless Romans by Terry Deary (Scholastic, 2003)

Historian
Studies the Roman occupation and the legacy of the Roman empire.

Custodian
Controls galleries and archaeological sites, and looks after displays so that members of the public can visit.

Conservationist
Works with museums to preserve mosaics, frescoes and other artefacts.

Actor
Plays Roman parts on screen or stage: you too can be Russell Crowe!

Documentary maker
Re-creates the Roman world on film or television.

Visit Lullingstone Villa: Eynsford, near Swanley, Kent DA4 0JA
Telephone: +44 (0) 1322 863467
www.english-heritage.org.uk

See the Mildenhall Treasure and other late Roman artefacts in the British Museum in London:
Great Russell Street, London WC1B 3DG
Telephone: +44 (0) 20 7323 8482
www.thebritishmuseum.ac.uk

Visit Pevensey Castle in East Sussex, one of the late Roman fortifications:
Pevensey, near Eastbourne, East Sussex BN24 5LE
Telephone: +44 (0) 1323 762604

Glossary

amphitheatre
A large stadium, such as the Colosseum in Rome, where audiences watched gladiator fights and sporting events.

aqueduct
A pipe or covered channel carrying water, sometimes flowing across the top of a viaduct.

archaeology
The study of the past using scientific analysis of material remains, undertaken by archaeologists.

arena
The central, sand-covered part of the amphitheatre where gladiator fights were held.

Augustus
A title held by all Roman emperors since the empire was established by Octavian in 27BCE; the emperor's wife was known as Augusta.

auxiliary
A non-Roman citizen who fought in the army.

barracks
A group of buildings housing military personnel and equipment.

BCE
Before Common Era: a non-religious dating system in which 1BCE is equivalent to 1BC (Before Christ).

Byzantine empire
The eastern successor to the Roman empire, ruled from its capital Constantinople (now Istanbul) until its eventual defeat by the Ottoman Turks in 1453.

Caesar
A title held by the emperor's designated heir or second-in-command.

CE
Common Era: a non-religious dating system in which CE1 is the equivalent to AD1 (Anno Domini).

centurion
The commander of a century of 80 (originally 100) men within a legion.

circus
An oblong racetrack where chariot races were held.

citizen
A native of a state. Originally, one had to be born in Rome to Roman parents to become a citizen, but from CE212, all free men within the empire could become Roman citizens.

classical
Anything relating to the civilizations and cultures of ancient Greece and Rome.

consul
The most senior government officer in republican Rome: two consuls were elected each year by the Senate to lead the Senate and command the Roman army; during the empire, the post became largely ceremonial.

Curia
The Senate House, where the Roman Senate met.

dictator
An unelected head of state, who rules a country by force. Under the republic the Roman Senate had the power during emergencies to appoint a dictator for up to six months; after Caesar's murder in 44BCE, the post of dictator was abolished.

empire
Several countries ruled by another country and its emperor; the Roman empire lasted from 27BCE to CE476.

Etruscans
A tribe living north of Rome whose civilization flourished between 800–400BCE; in its early days, Rome was ruled by Etruscan kings.

forum
A large and grand open space in the middle of Rome used for public meetings and events; every Roman town and city had its own forum.

freedman/woman
A former slave who had been freed by his/her master or who had bought his/her own freedom.

garrison
The troops who maintain or guard a military base or fortified frontier.

groma
A surveying instrument using hanging strings that were aligned to make sure a road was straight.

hypocaust
A central heating system consisting of stone pillars supporting the floor around which flowed hot air heated by a furnace.

infantry
Foot soldiers.

lararium
A small household shrine where statuettes of the household gods were kept and worshipped with daily prayers, gifts and offerings of food.

latifundia
A large agricultural estate run for profit and employing numerous slaves.

Latins
A tribe in central Italy, including the Romans, who lived in Latium.

legion
The main infantry unit of the Roman army, commanded by a legate and consisting of around 6,000 legionaries.

limites
Originally a trackway, the word later came to mean a military road with a line of forts forming a militarized frontier zone.

ludus
A school.

magistrate
An elected government official of Rome who had extensive legislative, legal, administrative and religious responsibilities in the city.

milestone
A stone pillar erected by the side of a road to indicate its distance from one city, erected every Roman mile (1.48km) or 1,000 paces.

mosaic
A picture or design made from small pieces of coloured glass or stone.

patrician
A rich Roman landowner who had huge power in the city.

plebeians
The common people of Rome, who initially had limited rights in the city even though they were citizens.

province
A region of the Roman empire outside Italy controlled by a governor.

republic
A country without a hereditary king or queen whose rulers are elected by the people; Rome was a republic from 510 to 27BCE.

Senate
The law-making parliament of Rome, initially composed of around 300 members at the start of the republic but rising to about 600 at the start of the empire.

tetrarchy
A system of government introduced by Emperor Diocletian in CE293 in which overall responsibility for the empire was shared between two senior (Augustus) and two junior (Caesar) emperors, headed by Diocletian.

viaduct
A bridge built to carry a road or aqueduct across a valley or river.

villa
A large country house.

Index

Acknowledgements

The publisher would like to thank the following for permission to reproduce their material. Every care has been taken to trace copyright holders. However, if there have been unintentional omissions or failure to trace copyright holders, we apologize and will, if informed, endeavour to make corrections in any future edition.

Key: *b* = bottom, *c* = centre, *l* = left, *r* = right, *t* = top

Cover *c* Art Archive (AA)/ Staatliche Glypothek Munich / Dagli Orti (DO); cover background Scala, Italy; 1 AA/ Museo Nazionale Terme Rome / DO; 2–3 Galleria d'Arte Moderna Rome / Dagli Orti; 4–5 Getty Imagebank; 7 Scala/ Musei Capitolini, Rome; 8 Getty NGS; 8–9*t* Bridgeman Art Library (BAL)/ Louvre, Paris; 8–9*b* Getty Taxi; 9*br* Corbis/ Loggia dei Lanzi, Florence; 10*l* British Museum (BM); 10*r* Corbis/ Gianni Dagli Orti; 11*tl* AKG, London; 11*tr* AA/ Archaeological Museum Naples / DO; 11*b* Corbis; 12*l* Corbis; 12–13*t* Scala/ Courtyard of the Corazze, Vatican, Vatican City; 12–13*c* Corbis; 12–13*b* Getty News; 13*t* AA/ Museo della Civilta Romana Rome / DO; 14*tl* AA / Archaeological Museum Naples / DO; 14*br* Scala/ Museo di Villa Giulia, Rome; 15*tl* Getty; 15*r* Getty Stone; 16*tl* Corbis/ Archivo Iconografico, S.A; 16–17*b* Corbis; 17*tr* Corbis; 18*tl* AA/ Archaeological Museum Milan / DO; 18 Getty Taxi; 18–19 Alamy; 19*tl* BAL/ Museo e Gallerie Nazionali di Capodimonte, Naples; 19 Getty Imagebank; 20–21 Corbis; 20*l* AA/ Archaeological Museum Naples / DO; 21*br* Corbis; 22*l* Werner Forman Archive; 22–23 BAL/ Villa Barbarigo, Noventa Vicentina; 23*tr* British Museum; 23*bl* Werner Forman Archive; 24 Corbis; 25 Getty Stone; 26–27 Alamy; 27 AA / National Museum Bucharest / DO; 28*l* BAL/ Romisch-Germanisches Museum, Cologne; 28*tr* AA / Museo della Civilta Romana Rome / DO; 28–29*b* Corbis; 29*tr* BAL/ Musee de la Poste, Paris; 30–31 AKG, London; 30*tl* Corbis; 31*tl* Corbis; 32*t* Scala/ Soprintendenza alle Antichita', Rome; 32–33 Corbis; 33*b* AA / Museo della Civilta Romana Rome / DO; 34*t* Corbis; 34*br* Corbis; 34–35*c* AA / Musée Lapidaire Avignon / DO; 35*b* Corbis; 36–37 Corbis; 38*tr* AA / Musée du Louvre Paris / DO; 38–39*b* Getty; 40*tl* AA/ Archaeological Museum Rabat / DO; 40*bl* AA/ Museo della Civilta Romana Rome / DO; 40*bc* AA/ Museo della Civilta Romana Rome / DO; 40*br* AA/ Museo della Civilta Romana Rome / DO; 41*l* AA/ Archaeological Museum Merida Spain / DO; 41*r* AA/ Archaeological Museum Ostia / DO; 41*tl* AA/ Musée du Louvre Paris / DO; 41*tr* AA/ Musée du Louvre Paris / DO; 42–43 Corbis; 42*b* Corbis; 43*b* Corbis; 44*tl* AKG, London; 44–45 Corbis; 45*t* Corbis; 46*tl* AKG, London/Lessing; 46*bl* AA/ Musée du Louvre Paris / DO; 46–47 AA/ Antiquarium Castellamare di Stabia Italy / DO; 47*tr* Scala/ Antiquarium of the Palatine, Rome; 47*br* Corbis; 48tl Corbis; 48–49 Corbis; 49*br* Corbis; 50 AA/ Musée du Louvre Paris / DO; 51 Getty Photographer's Choice; 52*l* AA/ Musée du Louvre Paris / DO; 52*c* Corbis; 52*b* AA/ Archaeological Museum Volos / DO; 52*r* Corbis; 53*tl* AA/ Goreme Cappadoccia Turkey / DO: 53*l* Corbis; 53*cl* AA/ Museo Capitolino Rome / DO; 54*bl* Scala; 54–55*t* BAL/ © New-York Historical Society, New York, USA; 55*tl* Scala; 55*b* Heritage Image Partnership, London; 56*tl* NASA; 56*b* Corbis; 56–57*t* Corbis; 57*tr* Corbis; 57*b* Corbis; 58*tl* AA/ Natural History Museum / Eileen Tweedy; 59 Scala; 60–61 Corbis; 64 Getty Taxi

The publisher would like to thank the following illustrators:
Steve Weston, Samuel Weston 12–13, 18–19, 20–21, 28–29, 30–31, 36–37, 38–39, 42–43, 48–49; Sebastien Quigley 26–27; Jurgen Ziewe 52–53

Captions for prelim photographs:
1 Quadriga (four-horse chariot), Roman silver coin, 1st century BCE, Museo Nazionale Terme, Rome; 2–3 The Death of Julius Caesar by Vincenzo Camuccini, painted 1793; 4–5 Hadrian's Wall, Northumberland